JOHANN SEBASTIAN BACH

CONCERTO

for 3 Harpsichords and Strings
für 3 Cembali und Streicher
C major/C-Dur/Ut majeur
BWV 1064

Edited by/Herausgegeben von
Arnold Schering

Ernst Eulenburg Ltd

London · Mainz · Madrid · New York · Paris · Tokyo · Toronto · Zürich

All rights reserved. No part of this publication may be reproduced, stored in a retrieval system, or transmitted in any form or by any means, electronic, mechanical, photocopying, recording or otherwise, without the prior written permission of Ernst Eulenburg Ltd., 48 Great Marlborough Street, London W1V 2BN.

J. S. BACH
Concertos for Three Harpsichords

J. S. Bach's concertos for two, three and four harpsichords were probably written because he was running the Collegium Musicum in Leipzig. There were many excellent harpsichordists among the students, including both of Bach's eldest sons, and he was not afraid of writing for three and four harpsichords because in those days it was so much easier than it is now to assemble such instruments in one room.

We know that most of the concertos for one and two harpsichords were originally written for violin, and some may have been arrangements of compositions by other people. But both the concertos for three harpsichords are thought to be by Bach, though this cannot be proved as the autographs have disappeared. For the same reason it cannot be proved that Bach originally wrote them for keyboard instruments. There is some doubt as to his having composed the middle movement of the D minor Concerto (see the article on Bach's concertos for three harpsichords by H. Boas in the *Bach-Jahrbuch* for 1913), but it is certain that the adaptations as they stand are Bach's. Both works were first published in 1845 and 1850 by F. K. Griepenkerl, and in 1885 they were included in Vol. 31, part 3, of the Bach Gesellschaft edition by Paul Graf Waldersee; this includes remarks about the identification of the copyist.

The present Miniature Score mainly follows the Bach Gesellschaft edition.

As regards the D minor Concerto it is doubtful if Bach meant the tutti passages in the Siciliano to be played as written by all three harpsichords. This would not accord with the conventions of the time. It is much more likely that only one of them played the continuo, accompanying with chords on the first and fourth quavers of each bar. In the Palschau MS (Berlin Staatsbibliothek P 242) the Siciliano is missing. In the last movement of this concerto the string bass part at bar 41 (and at similar places later) seems out of place, and may be a continuo part requiring yet another harpsichord.

In the Adagio of the C major Concerto there are four tutti passages (bars 1-49; 9-12; 24-27; 44-47) in which the MS source gives the same figured bass to all three solo instruments. This is obviously a mistake by the copyist. In these passages it was probably intended that only one harpsichord should play the continuo, and the present score is adapted accordingly. The realisation of the figured bass in small notes is the work of the editor.

In order to impress the audience with the ever-changing conversational character of the three solo instruments, they should be placed as far as possible away from each other.

Halle, a.d. Saale, 1923

Arnold Schering
(Translation revised 1970)

© 1976 Ernst Eulenburg Ltd., London

J. S. BACH
Konzerte für 3 Cembali

Die Entstehung der Konzerte für zwei, drei und vier Cembali von J. S. Bach wird mit gutem Grunde auf Anregungen zurückgeführt, die sich dem Meister bei der Leitung des akademischen Collegium Musicum in Leipzig ergeben. Unter den Studenten, denen in den dreissger Jahren auch seine beiden älltesten Söhne angehörten, befanden sich viele treffliche Cembalospieler, und da es damals leichter war als heute, mehrere Cembali ohne grosse Schwierigkeiten und Kosten zugleich aufzustellen, schreckte Bach selbst vor Konzerten für drei und vier Cembali nicht zurück.

Von den Konzerten für ein Cembalo und denen für zwei Cembali wissen wir, dass die meisten ursprünglich für Violine komponiert waren, einige vielleicht sogar als Bearbeitungen fremder Kompositionen anzusehen sind. Die beiden Konzerte für drei Cembali in d moll und C dur gelten bis heute als Originalkompositionen Bachs. Eine Entscheidung darüber, ob sie es wirklich sind, und ob die Cembalofassung die ursprüngliche ist, kann, da weder Autographe noch weitere Unterlagen vorhanden sind, vorläufig nicht getroffen werden. Ein begründeter Zweifel an der Urheberschaft Bachs wird nur gegenüber dem Mittelsatz des d moll-Konzerts erhoben werden mussen (vgl. die Studie über Bachs Konzerte für drei Cembali von H. Boas im Bach-Jahrbuch für 1913). Sicher ist jedenfalls, dass beide Bearbeitungen, so wie sie vorliegen von Bachs Hand stammen. Beide Stücke wurden zum erstenmal 1845 und 1850 von F. K. Griepenkerl veröffentlicht und alsdann 1885 von Paul Graf Waldersee in Band 31, 3 der Gesamtausgabe der Bachschen Werke aufgenommen, wo zugleich über die handschriftlichen Quellen berichtet ist.

Die vorliegende Fassung der ‚Kleinen Partitur-Ausgabe' stützt sich im wesentlichen auf die Ausgaben der Bach-Gesellschaft.

Zum d moll-Konzert ist Folgendes zu bemerken. Ob Bach im Siziliano die Tuttistellen wirklich von allen drei Cembali hat mitspielen lassen, wie die Vorlagen angeben, ist zweifelhaft. Dieser Manier entspricht nicht den Gepflogenheiten der Zeit. Man darf vielmehr annehmen, dass nur eins der drei Cembali mit stützenden und ausfüllenden Akkorden auf dem ersten und vierten Achtel als Generalbassinstrument fungiert hat. In der Palschauschen Handschrift (P 242 der Staatsbibliothek, Berlin) fehlt das Siziliano überhaupt. – Im letzten Satze des Konzerts fällt der bei Beginn des ersten Solos (1. Cembalo) und an ähnlichen Stellen mitgehende Streichbass auf. Er wird nur verständlich, wenn man ihn als Continuostimme auffasst, zu welcher ehemals ein weiteres (also viertes) Cembalo mit Akkompagnementcharakter getreten ist.

Im Adagio des C dur-Konzerts sind in den Vorlagen die vier Tuttistellen (Takt 1-4, 9-12; 24-27; 44-47) derart für die Soloinstrumente angeordnet, dass bei allen dreien nur der bezifferte Bass steht. Das beruht offenbar auf einem Missverständnis des Abschreibers. Gemeint ist wohl, dass an diesen Stellen nur eins der Cembali akkompagniert. In diesem Sinne ist hier verfahren worden. Die in kleineren Noten wiedergegebene Generalbassaussetzund rührt vom Herausgeber her.

Um dass geistvolle, unterhaltsame Wechselspiel der drei Soloinstrumente für den Zuhörer eindrucksvoll zu gesalten, empfiehlt es sich bei Aufführungen, die drei Cembali möglichst getrennt von einander aufzustellen.

Halle, a.d. Saale, 1923   Arnold Schering

Concerto

I

Johann Sebastian Bach
1685-1750

E.E. 3823

Ernst Eulenburg Ltd

4

6

E.E.3823

8

E.E.3823

E.E.3823

16

E. E. 3823

100

22

II

E. E. 3823

E. E. 3823

III

40

E.E. 3823

48

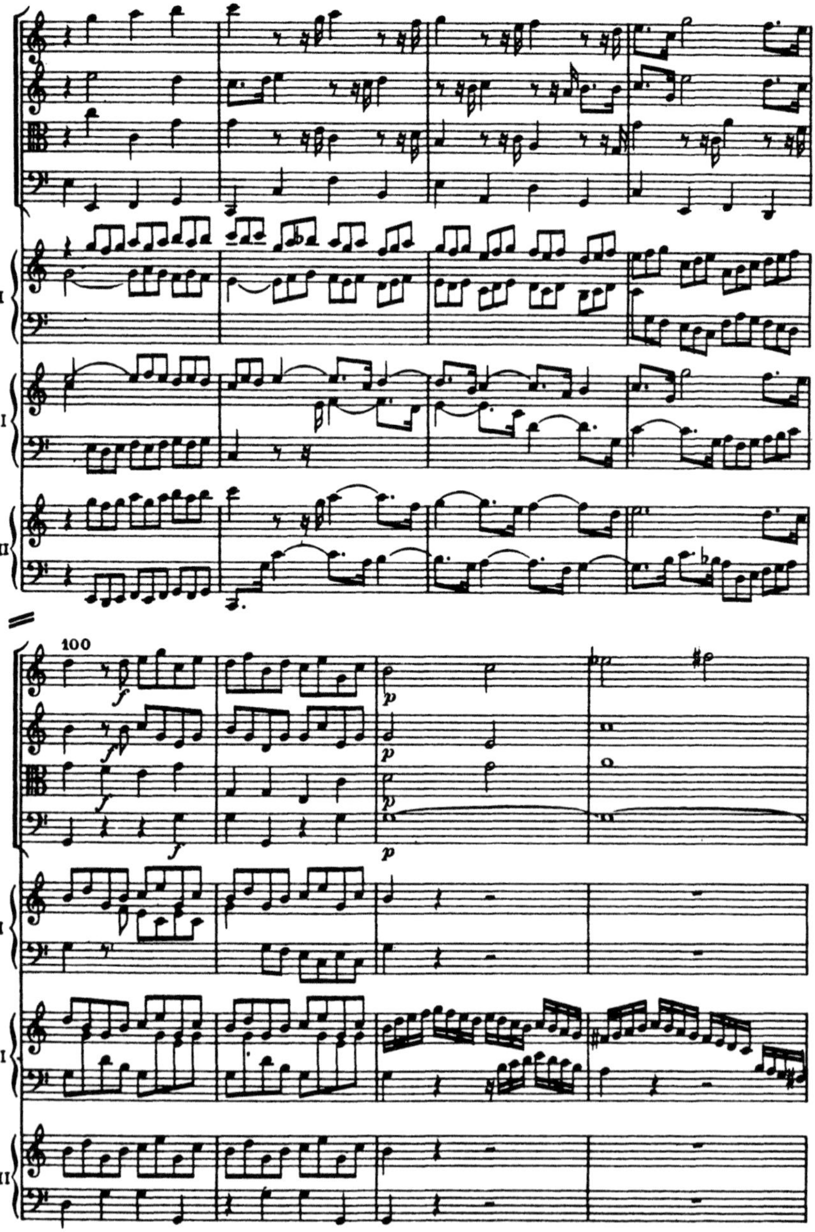
I
II
III
100
f
p
I
II
III

E.E.3823

140
tr

58

170

Violoncello

V.I

V.II

Vcl.

I

II

III